A YEAR IN THE LIFE OF THE CAIRNGORMS

A YEAR IN THE LIFE OF THE CAIRNGORMS

Chris Townsend

FRANCES LINCOLN LIMITED
PUBLISHERS

Frances Lincoln Ltd
4 Torriano Mews
Torriano Avenue
London NW5 2RZ
www.franceslincoln.com

British Library Cataloguing-in-Publication data
A catalogue record for this book is available from the British Library.

ISBN: 978-0-7112-3146-7

Printed and bound in China

9 8 7 6 5 4 3 2 1

half title page
A breeze ruffles Loch Mallachie. It is early
June and the land is green but in the
distance fresh snow brought on a north
wind covers the summit of Bynack More.

title page
The summit cliffs of Braeriach rising out of
high and remote Coire Bhrochain.

above right
The frozen summit of Ben Macdui coated
in snow and hoar frost.

CONTENTS

INTRODUCTION

The Landscape

The Cairngorms, a magnificent mountain range with vast alpine-arctic plateaux stretching out above cliff-rimmed corries, deep passes, long lochs, big rivers and the largest remnants of the ancient Caledonian forest, form the eastern bulwark of the Scottish Highlands. This is glorious country for any lover of wild nature.

The Cairngorms are a distinct block divided from the rest of the Highlands in the west by the Drumochter Pass, utilized by the A9 and the Perth to Inverness railway line. To the north, south and east, the hills fade away into low rolling heather moorland and then rich farmland.

The summits are all roughly the same height, between 800 and 1200 metres, as the Cairngorms form a massive dissected plateau which makes up the largest area of high ground in Britain (some 260 square kms over 800m). There are four main sections to this dissected plateau.

In the north the centrepiece is the Cairngorm Plateau itself, between Cairn Gorm and Ben Macdui, which at 20 square kms is the largest area of land above 1,000 metres in Britain. The Moine Mhor (great moss) plateau is to its west across the cleft of the Lairig Ghru pass, and the Ben Avon – Beinn a'Bhuirdh plateau to its east, across the Lairig an Laoigh pass.

To the south, across Deeside, lies the White Mounth and Glas Maol plateau – which contains Lochnagar, one of the best-known mountains in the Cairngorms – which continues westwards across the region known as the Mounth all the way to the Drumochter Pass. This southern high ground is crossed by only one road, the A93, in an east-west distance of 100kms. All these plateaux have undulating flat tops split by deep, steep-sided glens and passes, forming a distinctive and rugged landscape.

Five of the six highest mountains in Scotland are in the Cairngorms, all of them over 1,200 metres – Ben Macdui (1,309m, meaning MacDuff's hill), Braeriach (1,296m, brindled upland), Cairn Toul (1,291m, hill of the barn), Sgor an Lochain Uaine (1,258m, hill of the little green loch) and Cairn Gorm (1,244m, blue hill). There are 45 other summits over 914.4m (or 3,000ft), classified as Munros, named after Sir Hugh Munro who compiled the first *Tables of Heights Over 3,000 Feet* in 1891.

The Cairngorm mountains do not have any pointed, dramatic rock peaks and give a subdued, rolling look when viewed from a distance. But once you venture among the hills, the vast scale and the ruggedness of the corries and passes are hugely impressive. Below the hills the forests and lochs are wild and glorious, giving a suggestion as to what much of the Highlands were like before the glens were stripped of trees.

Rivers are a major feature of the lower areas of the Cairngorms, with two of the major rivers of Scotland – the Dee (Dhè – possibly a deity) and the Spey, both famous for their salmon fishing – running through the region.

The Dee could be said to be *the* river of the Cairngorms as it rises in the heart of the mountains, bubbling out of the ground near the summit of Braeriach, then crashing down the Falls of Dee into the great rocky bowl of An Garbh Choire (the rough corrie). The fast and furious young mountain stream then runs south down the Lairig Ghru (pass of oozing or gloomy pass) below Ben Macdui, picking up many other burns en route, before turning east and slowing, deepening and widening as it heads for Braemar, Balmoral and Ballater, the towns of Deeside. Here it winds through woods and meadows before leaving the hills and running through the lowland plain to Aberdeen and the sea.

The Spey holds itself more distant from the Cairngorms, running along the northern edge some way from the summits. Rising in hills to the west, it is already a sizeable river when it reaches the area, where it winds through a wide flood plain; either side are fields and woods stretching out towards the rippling line of the northern Cairngorms. As the Spey leaves the hill country it runs through whisky country, with many distilleries in the towns along the way. Strathspey, the wide valley of the river as it passes the Cairngorms, is the most populated part of the Cairngorms with many little towns like Aviemore, Grantown, Kingussie and Newtonmore. Tourism is the main business and the area is very busy in summer and during the ski season.

Many other rivers run from the heart of the mountains out into the straths (wide valleys) and glens. The Feshie (boggy meadow) starts high in the remote hills below the Minigaig Pass (mountains of the cleft pass), then twists and turns first east, then north, then west, then north again before finally joining the Spey east of Loch Insh. In Glen Feshie the river is wide and braided, running in multiple channels between gravel banks with ancient Caledonian pinewoods on either side, making one of the most magnificent glen landscapes in the Cairngorms.

Further east the Avon (simply the river or perhaps very bright one) has its source in the streams which pour down from the Cairngorm Plateau into Loch Avon, set in a long scoop sliced out of the mountains with steep and rocky slopes on either side, forming one of the most dramatic situations in the Cairngorms. From the loch, the River Avon runs east through remote little-visited heather moorland country with Ben Avon rising to the south, before turning north to Tomintoul and eventually, far from Loch Avon, to a confluence with the Spey on the north-eastern edge of the Cairngorms.

Lochs and lochans dot the landscape from the summits to the glens. At 1,120m, little Lochan Buidhe (yellow pool) on the Cairngorm Plateau is the highest named body of water in Britain. Not far to the south-west at 920m is the larger Loch Etchachan (loch of the juniper), set in a rocky bowl below big cliffs. Just north of Loch Etchachan and another 200 metres down is Loch Avon in its narrow mountain-sided trench. East of these lochs is Loch Einich (loch of the marsh) in a tremendous situation between the steep gully-riven crags of Sgor Gaoith (peak of the wind) and the western corries of Braeriach.

Of the many other lochs in high mountain corries one of the most significant is Lochnagar (loch of noise) which lies below the summit of the mountain to which it gave its name. On the south side of the mountain is the Dubh Lochan (the black pool) below the steep grim cliffs of Creag an Dubh-loch. The Dubh Lochan drains eastwards into the much bigger Loch Muick (loch of the pig), another loch in a deep trench between very steep hillsides.

Glen Muick is a long glen running south from Ballater in Deeside, which has no lochs of its own, whereas the much wider Strathspey has many. Big Loch Morlich (loch of the great slope) in Glen More, in a wonderful situation in a pine forest with a view to the northern Cairngorms, is perhaps the best known. Nearby is lovely An Lochan Uaine (the green pool) in Ryvoan Pass, hemmed in by steep pine and scree clad slopes. But arguably the most beautiful and romantic one of all is Loch an Eilein (the loch of the island) in Rothiemurchus

Forest (forest of Murchas's fort) set in magnificent pine forest with a backdrop of heather-clad hills and the ruins of a little castle, which dates back to the fourteenth century, on the island that gives the loch its name.

The Name

The original Gaelic name for the northern Cairngorms is Am Monadh Ruadh, which means the red mountains, a reference to the pinkish colour of the granite rocks in contrast to the Monadh Liath, the grey mountains, on the other side of Strathspey, which are built of a grey coloured rock called schist. Cairn Gorm – the blue mountain – was the name of two different hills, one above Glen More in Strathspey and one above Glen Derry on Deeside (these were local names, the fact that there was another Cairn Gorm not far away did not matter). The southern Cairn Gorm, being less well known, eventually had the prefix Derry added to distinguish it from its northern neighbour.

The Strathspey Cairn Gorm is clearly seen from Aviemore and other places in Strathspey and the first tourists in the nineteenth century started to use the name Cairngorms for the whole range – so the red mountains became the blue mountains. The name Am Monadh Ruadh has been revived in the Gaelic name for the Cairngorms National Park – Pàirc Nàiseanta a' Mhonaidh Ruaidh. During the twentieth century, the name Cairngorms was used to cover all the mountains east of the A9.

Before the name Cairngorms was applied to the whole range there was not a single local name for all the hills, though maps sometimes showed (and still show) the word Grampians spread across the region. However, on other maps, the word "Grampians" stretches all the way to the west coast. The exact location of "the Grampians", if there ever was one, and the meaning of the word are unknown, and many authorities point out that the name was never used by local people in the Cairngorms.

The name may date back to Mons Graupius, the name given by the Roman historian Tacitus in his *Life of Agricola* to the site of the battle where Agricola defeated the Picts around AD84. In the sixteenth century the name Grampius Mons appears on maps by Dutch, Swedish and Italian cartographers, with locations spread from the Monadh Liath north of the Cairngorms to the Borders far to the south. However Scottish maps of the following two centuries do not mention the name and it only reappears in the nineteenth and twentieth centuries.

The hills south of the River Dee, now commonly known as the southern Cairngorms, were known as Am Monadh, the mountain, which became the Scots mounth. The name mounth lives on in the White Mounth, a rounded summit south of Lochnagar, and the old tracks across the hills known as the Mounth Roads, which include the Capel Mounth (mounth of horses) from Glen Clova to Glen Muick, the Mounth Road and the Firmounth (mounth of pines), which both run from Glen Esk to Glen Tanar, and the Tolmount (mounth of the hollow), better known as Jock's Road, which runs

from Glen Doll in the Angus Glens over the hills to Glen Callater near Braemar on Deeside. (Tolmount is also the name of a summit lying close to Jock's Road).

Natural History

The harsh climate and exposed terrain of the high plateaux mean it has an arctic-alpine flora and fauna which is unique in Britain. Snow can lie for many months and strong winds sweep the plateaux regularly, and soil is thin and sparse.

Plants here are tiny and low, creeping across the ground and forming wind-resistant mats. Lichen, moss liverworts, grasses and sedges dominate the vegetation with patches of colour provided by flowers like moss campion. There are no trees or bushes, although in places dwarf willow, just a few inches high, may be found.

Below 750 metres, the vegetation changes and becomes richer and thicker with blaeberry, heather and longer grasses taking over. Around 650 metres the first stunted, wind blown trees appear – where there is a natural tree line that is. In most of the Cairngorms felling and overgrazing by deer and sheep has removed the high forest which slowly thins out with altitude, changing from full woodland to scattered scrub.

One of the few places still with a natural tree line is Creag Fhiaclach, above the mouth of Glen Feshie in the northern Cairngorms. Elsewhere though forest regeneration is taking place and trees can be seen advancing back up the hillsides. A good example is on the slopes of Meall a'Bhuachaille (hill of the herdsman) above Ryvoan Pass (pass of the slope of the bothy) between Glen More (big valley) and Abernethy Forest (forest of the mouth of the pure stream).

The natural Cairngorms forest is a boreal one of Scots pine and birch. The largest extent of this is in Strathspey, with the magnificent woodlands of the Abernethy, Glenmore, Rothiemurchus, Inshriach and Invereshie Forests. There are other smaller natural forest remnants in the Cairngorms, especially in Glen Lui, Glen Derry, Glen Quoich, Ballochbuie and Glen Tanar on Deeside. The removal of non-native plantations and a reduction in grazing pressure in

Reindeer have roamed the northern Cairngorms since the first herd was re-introduced in 1952. They are managed by the Reindeer Centre in Glenmore. They are smaller, more heavily built and paler than red deer. Both sexes have antlers.

recent years is allowing these forests to regenerate and spread. In the future the full glory of the Wood of Caledon may return to the Cairngorms.

While Scots pine and birch are the dominant trees, natural woodland may also contain aspen, rowan (a tough species that can be found clinging to the sides of high gorges), hazel, bird cherry, holly, alder, ash, oak, juniper and various willows. The fresh green of the newly-leaved deciduous trees is attractive in the spring but the real glory comes in the autumn when the birches turn brilliant gold, dotted with the red berries of rowan and bright yellow of aspen.

As well as the native species there are many plantations of Norway and Sitka spruce and European larch. Seed from these trees has spread beyond the regimented rows of the commercial forests and specimens may be found growing wild far from their source. Larches are especially noticeable in this respect as they turn a wonderful yellow, red and gold in the autumn and then lose their needles for the winter.

The high ground is home to birds only found on arctic-alpine terrain – ptarmigan, a member of the grouse family whose feathers turn white in winter; snow buntings, little black, brown and white birds often seen on summits seeking food scraps, and dotterel, delicate-looking plovers which run across the stones to draw you away from their nests. Golden eagles nest on crags and may be seen drifting overhead.

Lower down the hills live mountain hares, which also turn white in

winter, and red grouse, which explode out of the heather at your feet. Red deer may be seen grazing everywhere from the glens to the high tops when they are snow free. Originally forest animals, they have become adapted to the open hillsides.

Down in the forests there is a much wider variety of wildlife, and species rare elsewhere in Britain include crested tits, crossbills, capercaillie and red squirrels. On the lochs and rivers many species of waterfowl may be seen.

The most iconic bird of the Cairngorms is the osprey, which fishes in the lochs and rivers and nests in the forests. The osprey has nests in several places in the area now, but is best known from Loch Garten in Abernethy Forest in Strathspey, where it returned to breed in the 1950s after persecution drove it almost to extinction. The RSPB manages Loch Garten as part of the Abernethy Forest National Nature Reserve, which contains the largest single area of ancient Scots pine forest in Britain. The osprey nest can be observed from a purpose-built centre, (see www.rspb.org.uk/reserves/guide/l/lochgarten).

Another reintroduced species is the reindeer, which had been extinct for around 8,500 years until Mikel Utsi, a Swedish reindeer herder, brought them back in 1952 after noticing how the terrain was similar to that of Lapland where reindeer flourished. Now there are 150 reindeer in the northern Cairngorms. Semi-wild, they roam free and may be encountered in many areas. They can also be seen at the Reindeer Centre in Glenmore (www.cairngormreindeer.co.uk).

Geology

Around the high plateaux the underlying rock is Dalradian schist, formed from a mix of sedimentary rocks like sandstone, quartzite and shale that were laid down as sediments in an ancient ocean 700 million years ago. When this ocean, called Iapetus, began to close as the continents either side moved together some 460 million years ago, the sediments were compressed and buried deep below the surface where they were subject to extreme heat and pressure which changed them into metamorphic rocks. They were then forced upwards to form a great mountain chain known as the Caledonian Mountains.

At the end of this mountain-building process as the Iapetus Ocean finally closed around 425 million years ago, the force of the collision of continents melted rocks deep in the earth. These welled up towards the surface as liquid magma then cooled and solidified into the granite that makes up much of the high ground of the Cairngorms. Over tens of millions of years erosion wore down the Caledonian mountains to reveal this granite.

Much more recently, from around 2.6 million to 11,500 years ago, the glaciers of a series of Ice Ages sculpted the mountains, carving out the landforms we admire today. The deep cliff-rimmed corries and passes such as the Loch Avon basin and the Lairig Ghru were cut by the slow, grinding action of moving ice along already existing lines of weakness. The glaciers also dumped mounds of gravel and stones along their edges, seen today as rounded moraines, and cut deep "kettle" holes that filled up with water to form lochs such Loch Morlich.

The highest summits are likely to have been less glaciated than the corries and glens as the granite tors which dot them – especially Ben Avon (hill of the river), Beinn Mheadhoin (middle hill) and Bynack More (possible big cap) – were not worn away by the ice. The plateaux glaciers were on gently sloping or flat ground and so moved very slowly, which reduced their erosive power, while the glaciers on the steep slopes of the corries and passes moved faster and more forcefully.

The result is the huge contrast between the undulating plateaux and the steep-sided corries, passes and glens which cut into and through them. As the glaciers melted, powerful rivers ran below the ice, carrying rocks and boulders and carving meltwater channels running across the grain of the hills, such as the Chalamain Gap (ravine of the corrie of the assembly) between Glen More and the Lairig Ghru. The glaciers deposited vast amounts of sand and gravel in the glens, which can be seen in high banks cut by today's rivers in places like Glen Feshie.

Since the last glaciers vanished from the high corries erosion has continued as rain, snow, ice, frost and wind slowly wear down the hills. The large boulder fields found on the plateaux (known as blockfields), which can make walking so difficult, were formed by ice and frost working into cracks and crevices in the granite bedrock and causing it to shatter. On the steep walls of passes and glens like the Lairig Ghru, Gleann Einich and Glen Feshie, rain and snow can saturate the ground and cause it to slip downhill, forming gullies often with scree fans of debris at their base.

July storm clouds gathering over Carn Etchachan, the Shelter Stone Crag and the head of Loch Avon.

History

The Scottish Highlands as a whole were very remote and little visited by outsiders until the nineteenth century. However, the Cairngorms were more accessible than some other areas, and do not appear to have been quite as unknown as the rest of the Highlands, with descriptions of the area going back to the 1600s.

Ian R. Mitchell in *Scotland's Mountains Before the Mountaineers* (1988) points out that three long wide glens run into the Cairngorms from the lowlands to the east – those of the rivers Dee, Don and Spey – and that tracks linking the lowland regions of central Scotland and the north-east crossed the hills. Mitchell tells the story of John Taylor, a Thames bargeman known as the Water Poet, who travelled to the area in 1618 and went up Deeside to the Braes of Mar from where he saw Ben Avon. Taylor also saw wolves, soon to be extinct, and many big trees, suggesting the area was much more heavily wooded than now.

Before the mid-eighteenth century the Highlanders lived in clans – extended families – and owed loyalty to the clan chief. The chief's wealth lay in land and people rather than money. This was not a cash economy. The clansmen were duty bound to take up arms at the chief's command and over the centuries there was much warfare between clans and over who should rule Scotland and, after James VI of Scotland became James I of England in 1603, England as well.

After the Stuart dynasty came to an end in 1688 when James VII of Scotland and II of England was forced from the throne, many of the clans supported attempts to restore James's son, also called James and known as the Old Pretender. This led to the unsuccessful Jacobite (from the Latin for James) uprisings of 1715 and 1745 and to great changes for the Highlands, including the end of the clan system. After the 1715 rebellion General Wade built the first real roads in the Highlands for troops to use. In the Cairngorms the main road went over the Drumochter Pass to Badenoch and Strathspey along the route now followed by the A9. Many forts were built too. The impressive remains of one of these, Ruthven Barracks, can be seen on a hillock just outside Kingussie in Strathspey.

But Wade's roads, forts and soldiers did not prevent the second rebellion of 1745, when the clans rallied to the Old Pretender's son, Charles the Young Pretender, better known as Bonnie Prince Charlie. This uprising ended in disaster for the Jacobites with defeat at the Battle of Culloden, north of the Cairngorms near Inverness, in 1746, which was followed by the persecution of the clans involved. Initially many Jacobites were killed or imprisoned, their chiefs fled abroad, their land was seized by the government and the raising of private armies was banned. Tartan, the kilt and other symbols of the clan were also proscribed.

At the same time as this breaking of the clans the nascent Industrial Revolution was bringing huge changes to the south, in Lowland Scotland and England, and the Highlands had products needed there – cattle, timber and, increasingly, sheep. Drovers took cattle through the high passes of the Cairngorms – Lairig an Laoigh means the pass of the calves – to markets down south, and the forests were felled and the timber floated down the Dee and the Spey.

Then came the sheep, needed to supply wool for the mills of the newly-industrialized towns. Land which been held communally by the clans was sold for sheep farming. There was no space for sheep and people and only a few shepherds were needed. The people, betrayed by their chiefs, had to leave to find work and sustenance. Many who chose not to were driven away or even burnt out of their homes. Sheep were worth money but people were not. The clan chiefs, whose lands had been returned to them in the early 1780s, were now part of the British aristocracy and wanted cash not armies. For nearly a century from 1780 the clearance of people from the Highlands continued.

As these changes took place map makers, scientists and the first tourists started to arrive in the Cairngorms. In 1764 the founder of modern geology, James Hutton, visited Glen Tilt where he found proof in the bed of the River Tilt that granite was forced up into older rocks from below. Many of the early visitors were not so serious-minded. Ian Mitchell tells of a Colonel Thornton who made a hunting tour, probably in 1786, during which he visited Glen Feshie from where he crossed the hills to Gleann Einich. Thornton

Red deer are forest animals that have adapted to life on the open hill due to the great reduction in forest cover. The name comes from their reddish coloured summer coat. This is shed in the autumn and replaced by a thicker duller coloured winter coat. The male red deer, called stags, grow new antlers every year. The female hinds do not have antlers.

A later painter connected with the romanticism of the Cairngorms was Sir Edwin Henry Landseer, famous for *The Monarch of the Glen*, a painting of a red deer stag. Landseer did some painting in Glen Feshie, including preliminary sketches for *The Monarch of the Glen*, and in 1861 Queen Victoria, who was very keen on his paintings, visited a hut there to look at a fresco of stags by him. This building is gone now with just a tall chimney remaining. Seton Gordon in the *Highways and Byways in the Central Highlands*, published in 1949, says the remains of the frescoes could still be seen then. Gordon calls the building a chapel but in her journals Queen Victoria describes it as a hut.

Victoria and Prince Albert were keen on deer stalking and this soon became fashionable with the aristocracy. On the hills sheep were replaced by deer as stalking estates replaced sheep farms. Red deer were native to the Cairngorms anyway but their numbers were increased by introductions and the killing of predators and have remained artificially high in many areas ever since, leading to over-grazing and a lack of regeneration in the forests.

Better roads and then railways made the Cairngorms more accessible to visitors in the nineteenth century. The railway arrived at Aviemore in Strathspey in 1863 and Ballater on Deeside in 1866, making travel to the Cairngorms faster and more comfortable and attracting an ever-increasing number of tourists.

Mountaineering as a leisure activity had begun in the 1850s with English visitors to the Alps and soon spread to the Cairngorms. In 1887 the first hillwalking and climbing club in Scotland, the Cairngorm Club, was founded at the Shelter Stone, a vast boulder with room to sleep underneath it, above Loch Avon. The Cairngorms have remained a major destination for outdoor pursuits ever since. In the second half of the twentieth century Glenmore Lodge, Scotland's National Training Centre, was established in Glen More near Loch Morlich and the ski resorts at Cairn Gorm, Glen Shee and the Lecht were constructed.

Access to the hills was an issue from the early days of tourism as many landowners wanted to keep their estates private. Various legal battles were fought over access rights. One of the earliest was in 1847 when a Professor Balfour and a party of botanists were barred

said the mountains here were 31,000 feet high! Others soon followed Thornton, and the first account of an ascent of Cairn Gorm, made in 1801, comes from a Mrs Sarah Murray, who wrote a guide to Scotland.

The popularity of the Cairngorms grew through the early 1800s and then took off when Queen Victoria gave them her seal of approval. Victoria first visited the area in 1842 and fell in love with the Highlands. Ten years later she purchased Balmoral where she had a new castle built. Royal Deeside was soon established as a major tourist destination (Mitchell calls this 'the Balmorality' and says that Deeside was "saturated by the presence of the British monarchy"). Victoria travelled all over the Cairngorms, climbing many of the hills. Her journeys are recorded in Mitchell's interesting and entertaining book *On the Trail of Queen Victoria in the Highlands*.

The romantic view of the Highlands, encouraged by Victoria, can be traced back to the novels and poems of Sir Walter Scott and to artists who painted dramatic Highland landscapes, such as those of George Fennel Robson, published in his book *Scenery of the Grampian Mountains* in 1814. Ian Mitchell says that these paintings "though romantically exaggerated ... give us the fullest visual picture to that date of the Cairngorms".

from going up Glen Tilt by the Duke of Atholl. A subsequent court case by the Association for the Protection of Public Rights of Roadway, founded in 1845, which later became the Scottish Rights of Way and Recreation Society, confirmed that there was a right of way up the glen.

Another court case occurred in 1888 after the owner of Glen Doll tried to close Jock's Road, a route from the glen over the hills to Glen Callater and Deeside. Again the Scottish Rights of Way and Recreation Society fought successfully for the right of access, showing that drovers had used Jock's Road to take their beasts to market and so it was an established right of way.

By the late twentieth century access problems had eased and in 2003 a legal right of access was granted in the Land Reform Act.

Continuing deforestation, the replacement of native woods with plantations, over-grazing, bulldozed roads, ski resort expansion and other developments slowly degraded the environment, although the core of the area remained wild and beautiful. This began to change at the end of the twentieth century with changes in the Forestry Commission whereby it finally recognized the value of natural woodland. There was also an increase in land ownership by conservation bodies, with the RSPB taking over the Abernethy Forest estate in Strathspey and the National Trust for Scotland taking over the Mar Lodge estate on Deeside. This reflected a growing understanding of the importance and need for biodiversity and wild places.

Then in 2003 the Cairngorms National Park was created (www.cairngorms.co.uk). At 4,528 square kilometres, this is the largest national park in Britain, and in 2010 the park was extended to include Blair Atholl, Glen Tilt, Beinn a'Ghlo, Glen Shee and Killiekrankie in the south-west of the region.

The existence of the park should ensure that the unique beauty and wildness of the Cairngorms will be there for future generations to enjoy, though there are still threats from developments like wind farms, electricity pylons, bulldozed roads and more. All who love the wild Cairngorms should be prepared to work with conservation bodies for its preservation and, where necessary, restoration.

The Weather

Lying on the east side of the Highlands the Cairngorms have less rainfall than the hills to the west – considerably less than those on the West Coast – though it can still rain heavily for days on end. The glens and straths are drier than the hills too, especially those to the north and east. Strathspey can be in bright sunshine when the northern Cairngorms are hidden in wet cloud. There is a weather station on the summit of Cairn Gorm and rainfall readings show that around three times as much rain falls there than in the valleys.

The prevailing winds are south-westerly and these are relatively mild and usually bring rain rather than snow. However winds do blow from the north and east, especially in the winter. These cold winds reach the Cairngorms before the rest of the Highlands and often bring snow, which can be heavy. In most years the Cairngorms have more snow than anywhere else in the Highlands, which explains why three of Scotland's five ski resorts are found in the region. On the summits snow can lie for over 100 days a year and patches can remain in high deep gullies all year round.

Snow can fall in any month, though in June, July and August it is rare and when it does fall it is usually just a dusting on the highest summits which melts very quickly. Late September can see snow settling on the tops – I have been ski touring on the Cairngorm Plateau then – although this is unusual and most years it is October that sees the first heavy falls.

Mild southerly winds can strip snow quickly, especially at low levels, and there can be a succession of snowfalls and thaws between October and May, when the final melt usually occurs. This means the hills can be virtually snow free in December and January but snow covered in April. At low levels, February is the month when snow lies longest in most years, though sometimes there can be three months of snow cover in the glens, as happened in the winter of 2009–10.

When the snow lies deep avalanches can be a hazard. One of the earliest known avalanche disasters took place in the Gaick Pass in the western Cairngorms in January 1800, when a bothy in which a party of deer hunters was sheltering was destroyed, killing all the

inhabitants. Sadly, many people have died in avalanches since then. There is now an avalanche information system with daily updates through the winter for the northern and southern Cairngorms (www.sais.gov.uk).

High in the hills mist or low cloud is often present and can sweep in quickly, reducing visibility and making navigation difficult. These mists are often damp and in sub zero temperatures can condense on rocks and stones, forming long frost feathers which are both exotic and beautiful. Over many days this frost can build up into thick overlapping plates.

As well as being rainy and snowy, the Cairngorms are windy, with 160kph (100mph) winds occurring on the hills on many occasions through the winter months of October and May. The Cairngorm Weather Station recorded the highest wind speed in Britain on March 20, 1986, 278kph (173mph). Passes funnel winds too, which sometimes makes them windier than the summits above.

The combination of wind, snow and low cloud can result in extremely difficult and dangerous conditions on the hills when standing can be almost impossible, progress slow and the cold bitter. There have been many accidents in such weather over the years and all walkers and mountaineers should be properly equipped and have the necessary skills, including the ability to navigate in a white-out. Checking weather forecasts before heading out is always a good precaution. Daily weather forecasts are available from the Mountain Weather Information Service for the Cairngorms National Park (www.mwis.org.uk) and from the Met Office for the East Highlands (www.metoffice.gov.uk/loutdoor/mountainsafety). Further inform-ation on mountain safety can be had from the Mountaineering Council of Scotland (www.mcofs.org.uk/mountain-safety.asp).

In summer temperatures can be quite warm – in the upper twenties degrees celsius in the glens – but the Cairngorms are more noted for cold than heat. Hard frosts and sub zero temperatures are common in the winter with January and February being the coldest months. Braemar on Deeside is particularly chilly. The coldest temperature in Scotland, a bitter -27 degrees celsius, has been recorded there twice, on February 11, 1895 and January 10, 1982.

Chapter 1:
Spring

Looking down from the plateau to the deep blue of Loch Avon in the heart of the Cairngorms.

Spring comes slowly in the Cairngorms, especially in the high country. There is a long delay between the first lengthening hours of daylight in February and the fading of winter. The Met Office definition of spring as the period between March 1 to May 31 is meaningless here. Even the traditional start on the spring equinox – around March 21 – can seem far too early on the snowbound mountains. Snow often lies deep in March and this is a good month for winter sports – skiing and snow and ice climbing.

Often the snow lasts well into April too, shrinking only slowly back up to the highest ground and into the deepest gullies. Sunny days in April can feel spring-like though, as the sun has a power not felt for six months. By May the snowpack has lessened and there are signs of brightness in the vegetation as the sparse plants on the plateaux

start to grow, though it is June before a sweep of brighter colour suffuses the stony landscape.

Down in the forests and glens spring is well-established by May. Moorland birds – curlews, lapwing and oystercatchers – return to their breeding grounds in March and their wild calls are often the first sign of the change of the seasons. Late in the month the ospreys return from their wintering grounds in Africa to Loch Garten and other nests. Other birds are singing and the silence of the winter woods is broken.

In April buds appear on the birches and rowans and towards the end of the month the first fresh green leaves can be seen. May is the month of forest brightness and spring colour though, with flowers on the woodland floor and deciduous trees in full leaf. Out in the

A calm April day at Loch Mallachie, which lies in the largest remaining fragment of the old Caledonian pine forest in the RSPB's Abernethy Forest Nature Reserve. To the south snow on the mountains acts a reminder that winter still lingers on the high tops.

Late afternoon sun breaks through the clouds over the snow-clad ridges of the northern Cairngorms.

On the Cairngorm Plateau looking towards Cairn Gorm. It is late April but the snow still lies deep.

meadows and on the moors the brown of winter is slowly being replaced by new green grass and burgeoning blaeberry. Cuckoos call loudly from trees.

By June spring has taken over and the land is green. Only on the high tops do the last traces of snow give a reminder of the past winter. Ptarmigan in their mottled grey summer plumage scurry across the snow-free ground, well-camouflaged against the mottled stones.

May and June, the prime spring months, are wondrous times to be in the Cairngorms. These are the driest months and often the air is sharp and clear with the landscape sparkling in the sunshine. Warmth permeates the land, a relief after the cold of winter, and there is an anticipation of the warm days of summer to come.

An orange glow suffuses the eastern sky after sunset in late April as the temperature falls and the sun-softened snow freezes hard and icy on Stob Coire an t-Sneachda on the northern edge of the Cairngorm Plateau.

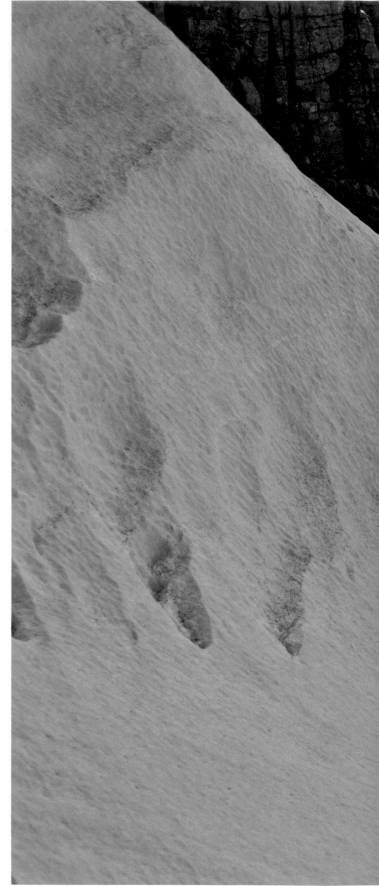

May Day on Stob Coire an t-Sneachda. The snow has gone from the corrie floor and the lochan is ice-free but there are still big drifts in the gullies and high on the corrie walls.

previous pages The Pools of Dee in the heart
of the Lairig Ghru in early June.

The River Spey meandering
through Strathspey in late April.
The land is slowly greening over.

The River Feshie roaring down
Glen Feshie carries away the last of
the winter's snow.

Little Ryvoan Bothy in the northern
Cairngorms sits amid heather-clad
slopes with only a few patches of grass
showing the colours of the coming
spring even though it is mid-April.

The summit of Cairn Lochan in the northern Cairngorms in early May. The steep rocks of the cliffs above Coire an Lochain are bare, but big drifts still remain in the gullies and on shaded slopes.

On a bright May day above Glen Clunie in the southern Cairngorms the Allt a' Gharbh-choire drains the slopes of Carn an Tuirc, which rises, dappled white and grey with snow and scree, in the background.

A double rainbow curves over Glen Feshie as May storms sweep across the landscape.

The Cairnwell Burn runs under an old stone bridge in Glen Clunie with the brown slopes above showing little sign of spring, even though it is mid-May.

The fresh spring green of birches newly in leaf spreads up the lower hillside of waterfall-splashed Mullach Clach a'Bhlair in Glen Feshie.

The River Dee winds through fresh green meadows past Mar Lodge in Upper Deeside.

Late May at the trig point and viewfinder on the Cac Carn Beag, the summit of Lochnagar.

A rainbow arcs over Loch Muick in the southern Cairngorms as a spring squall dampens the hillside.

Carn Liath on Beinn A'Ghlo rises above green fields and woods and the bright white of Blair Castle on the southern edge of the Cairngorms.

On a perfect sunny spring day, the unspoilt south side of Cairn Gorm rises out of the deep trench containing Loch Avon.

Looking down the great cliffs of Lochnagar to the loch after which the mountain is named. A wash of spring green spreads across the corrie floor.

The last snowmelt on the Cairngorm
Plateau speeds away in the waters of
the Feith Buidhe and the Garbh Uisge
Beag below the great Shelter Stone
Crag and tor-dotted Beinn Mheadhoin.

The rocks and cliffs of the Chalamain Gap, a meltwater channel cut by a boulder-filled stream which rushed beneath a glacier in the last Ice Age. The rowan trees and blaeberry bushes push up through spaces between the boulders, bright with new spring growth.

Looking down the River Dee in the Lairig Ghru from the slopes of Ben Macdui. The hills are still brown in early June, with little sign of the coming spring.

Chapter 2: Summer

Looking down the cliffs of Cairn Lochan to the Lochan far below. White streaks of water from recent rains rush down distant slopes.

Summer is the season of greenness, holidaymakers, rain – and midges. The sun is high in the sky and the days are warm. They are often hazy too, with distant hills reduced to pale silhouettes against a pale sky. Humidity is high and there is usually more rainfall than in spring. Still, there are days when the sky is clear and the sun sharp, the rocks dry and warm to the touch, and the views crystal clear.

Life burgeons in glorious abandon and in July and August, the months of high summer, the hills are coated with a green wash of growth. In the woods and meadows the grass is long, the bracken almost impenetrable, and there are flowers everywhere. The fresh bright green of spring has darkened into a less colourful but more solid green that gives substance and depth to the landscape.

The birds are feeding their young and singing less – the rivalry for mates is over. The cuckoo is silent, a relief to campers who are no longer disturbed by its loud dawn calls. At Loch Garten, the young ospreys are stretching their wings and preparing for flight. Heather

The sharp point of Sgor an Lochain Uaine rises above the fresh summer grass on the floor of the huge An Garbh Choire, which bites deep into the hills from the Lairig Ghru pass.

A double rainbow curves over the ancient Caledonian pine woods of Glen Quoich to the north of Deeside during a late June storm.

The huge Shelter Stone Crag rises above scattered scree and boulders in the Loch Avon basin. On the right is the Shelter Stone, which has been in use for hundreds of years and below which half a dozen or more people can sleep.

starts to spread its distinctive purple over the moors and lower hills in August, reaching a peak at the end of the month and in early September.

Humidity and heat bring greenness and prolific life, including the midges, the most annoying and painful wildlife in the Cairngorms. Often abundant at dawn and dusk on calm days, midges can make being outdoors unbearable unless you keep moving. Wind and bright sunshine deter them, as does heavy rain. Insect repellent, head nets and tightly-woven clothing can be as essential in summer as an ice axe is in winter.

Summer is short in the Cairngorms. By late August the first hints of autumn colour start to appear on the trees. In September summer migrant birds leave. The Loch Garten ospreys follow the sun southwards, heading for their winter feeding grounds in Africa. The days start to draw in and thoughts are of the long dark nights to come rather than the endless days of June.

View from the cliffs of Stob Coire an t-Sneachda to Cairn Gorm on a bright summer's day.

Red deer blend in well against the dull browns of moorland hills. The winter coats of these stags are just beginning to moult.

View from Braeriach across the bright
green summer floor of An Garbh Choire
to the Lairig Ghru, Ben Macdui (left),
Cairn Toul and Sgor an Lochain Uaine.

Looking across An Garbh Choire from Braeraich to Cairn Toul and Sgor an Lochain Uaine, with Lochan Uaine itself nestled between them in its high hanging corrie.

The infant River Dee starts its journey to the sea high on the slopes of Braeriach. At the height of summer grass and moss cover the thin soil of the high plateau.

The waters of the Allt Coire Dhondail provide moisture for a rich vegetation of moss and grass high on the slopes of Braeriach, as the burn starts its descent to Loch Einich far below. The steep slopes of Sgoran Dubh Mor rise above the loch.

Waterfalls on the Allt Coire Dhondail as it descends a gully on Braeriach.

The Am Beanaidh running through heather-covered moraines in Gleann Einich. Braeriach rises in the distance.

A shallow pool in Rothiemurchus Forest
is bright with summer growth.

A lone ancient pine tree marks the
farthest reach of the forest in Gleann Einich.

A finger of rough granite points into the sky high on the slopes of Beinn a'Bhuird.

The granite landscape on Beinn a'Bhuird under cirrus clouds marking approaching wet weather. Within four hours, rain was falling.

The vista of the northern Cairngorms. Loch Morlich and Glenmore
Forest as seen from Meall a'Bhuachaille above Glen More.

The view over Loch Morlich and Glenmore Forest to the Northern Corries of Cairn Gorm.

Evening light on Loch Morlich and Glenmore Forest, with Stob Coire an t-Sneachda and Cairn Lochan on the horizon. Out on the loch, canoeists enjoy the balmy summer evening.

Mid-July and the hills are at the height of their summer greenness. The view from Sgor Gaoith over Loch Einich to Braeriach.

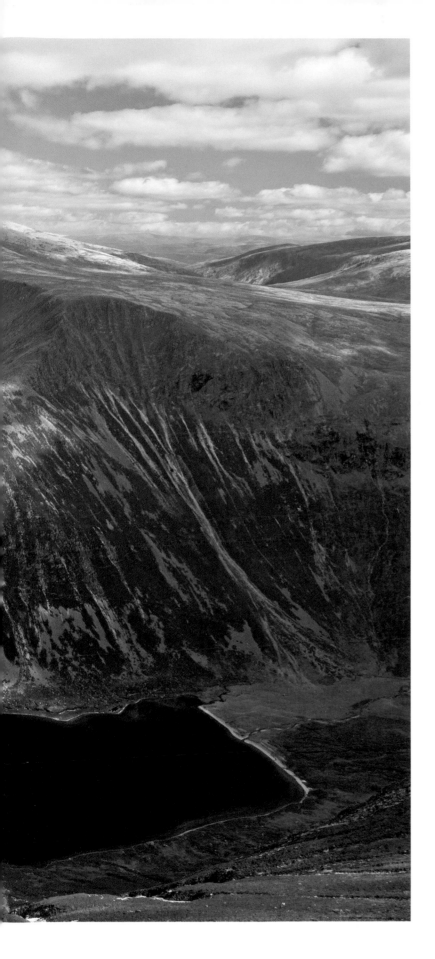

Rich green slopes run down to Loch Einich in its narrow glacial trench between the stony slopes of Sgor Gaoith and Braeriach.

Beinn Mheadhoin and the crags of Stacan Dubha rising above Loch Avon on a warm July day.

Looking through a gap in the cliffs of Coire Sputan Dearg on Ben Macdui to the isolated stony summit of Derry Cairngorm. Once just called "Cairn Gorm", the 'Derry', named from the glen to its east, was added to distinguish it from the much better known Cairn Gorm above Glen More and Strathspey.

The complex ice-carved topography of the Loch Avon basin with Beinn Mheadhoin, Stacan Dubha, Carn Etchachan and the Shelter Stone Crag rising high above.

Swirling clouds over the tiny pointed summit of Sgor Gaoith, rising above the wide high plateau of the Moine Mhor.

The first purple of heather appears in mid-July in the mouth of Coire Garbhlach above Glen Feshie.

View across Coire nan Clach from Beinn a'Bhuird to the vast tor-dotted plateau of Ben Avon.

63

The placid River Spey winds through peaceful late summer meadows and woods at Grantown on-Spey.

A fiery summer dawn at Loch Einich.

Chapter 3:
Autumn

Autumnal storm light at dusk in Strathspey, with the Hills of Cromdale shrouded in cloud.

Autumn creeps in slowly, advancing in hints and warnings during September; the first suggestions of red and gold on the trees, the first frosts – often just a faint, brief skim of white on the grass – the fading of the flowers, the decline in bird song. Towards the end of the month the heather is losing colour fast, the dense bracken has turned orange and is beginning to thin and collapse, and the berries hang thick and scarlet on the rowans. The shorter days and longer nights are noticeable now.

October is the first real month of autumn. The woodland colours are in their full glory – huge splashes of gold and red against the dark green of the pines. Birches are the brightest colours in the palette in this brilliant display, with their orange and yellow leaves. Dotted among them are the reds of rowan and cherry and the purer yellow of aspen. In some years this show can last for several weeks, but all too often the first autumn gales rip the dying leaves from the trees and cast them on the woodland floor to form a colourful mosaic.

The storms are colder now, the rain often holding hints of sleet and snow. Sometimes the first snow is on the tops late in September, but more usually it is October which sees the first falls, with perhaps a brief dusting at low levels. Ice appears on the edges of the high lochans. The hills turn brown and grey again; the brief greening of summer over.

The essential sound of autumn in the Cairngorms is the roaring of the red deer stags, for this is the rutting season when they compete for hinds. Their guttural bellowing is wild and raucous, echoing across the hillsides. Overhead skeins of geese cross the sky, coming in to feed in the meadows and marshes. On the hills the ptarmigan and mountain hares start to change into their white winter coats, both suddenly highly visible when there is no snow.

During November, autumn becomes winter. The leaves fall from the trees, their colours faded. Frosts are more common and heavier. Snow falls more thickly on the summits and lingers longer. Daylight hours are short and conditions on the hills can be harsh, whether from blizzards or cold rain driven on near-freezing winds.

A subdued October day in Strathspey with aspen and birch showing autumn tints and the distant Cairngorms purple under a weak sun and hazy sky.

The leaves of wind-gnarled aspen in Strathspey show that autumn is truly underway.

A closer view of the rainbow and storm over Glen Rinnes.

Wild storm light over Glen Rinnes, viewed from Creagan a'Chaise in the Hills of Cromdale in the north-east corner of the Cairngorms.

A dense bank of cloud creeps across the
Moine Mhor towards Braeriach.

Autumn storms fill this stream draining Coire an Lochain. Cairn Lochan rises in the distance.

A cold bright autumn day on the Moine Mhor
looking across Gleann Einich to Sgor Gaoith and
Sgoran Dubh Mor. The grasses are yellowing now
and fading towards their winter tan.

Remnants of the first snowfall of the autumn cling
to the slopes of Braeriach. On the left the
snowmelt-filled waters of the young River Dee pour
down the crags.

The green of the grasses is fading beside the infant River Dee as it slides over granite stones towards the lip of An Garbh Choire. On the left a scattering of new snow can be seen high on Ben Macdui, with the shadowed face of Cairn Toul across the Lairig Ghru to the right

A birch wood is a wash of yellow and gold in a hidden defile in the forests of Strathspey.

Red rowan berries and yellow birch leaves in Strathspey.

Late afternoon light illuminates the autumn colours of a wood in Strathspey after a passing storm. In the distance the edge of the Hills of Cromdale hang dark against the clouds.

A view over the woods of Strathspey to the Hills of Cromdale in late October. Some birches have already lost their leaves and the orange bracken is fading fast.

Fresh snow covers the Hills of Cromdale
rising above the brown and gold-tinted
autumn fields and woods of Strathspey.

Mid-November and a fringe of ice runs
round Loch Gamhna in Rothiemurchus
Forest. Snow dusts the crags above and lies
more thickly on the highest tops.

A cold autumn day at Loch an Eilein in
Rothiemurchus Forest, with the snow-
dusted hills of Cadha Mor, Creag Dhubh
and Creag Fhiaclach rising above the trees.

Late November and Lochan Deo in Rothiemurchus Forest is almost frozen over, with fresh snow lying on the ice.

By early December the larches
are bare beside the Falls of Bruar
at the foot of Glen Bruar in the
southern Cairngorms.

Shafts of sunlight cut through storm clouds to light up a wind-ruffled Loch Morlich.

New snow on the glacier-scraped flanks of Bynack More, rising out of Strath Nethy.

After dusk in late autumn with the sun lighting up the swirling clouds above the dark hills of Strathspey.

High in the mountains in November, winter has arrived. Looking across Glen Avon to Beinn Mheadhoin from the slopes of Cairn Gorm.

Chapter 4:
Winter

Cracks appear in the ice on part-frozen Loch Muick, with Creag Bhiorach rising above the far shore.

Winter is the long season in the Cairngorms, sometimes beginning as early as October and often running into April. December, January and February are the deep midwinter months though – dark, cold and monochrome.

It is barely light at nine in the morning and dark by four in the afternoon. Trips to the hills need to be carefully planned to use the short hours of daylight. Descents by headlamp in the dark are not unusual. Temperatures hover around freezing. Just above zero and there is chilling rain and grey windswept clouds which suck all colour out of the land and all warmth out of your body. When the temperatures drop below zero the land is bound hard under snow, frost and ice .

But it is brighter too, the whiteness of snow and ice shining even on dull days. In sunshine the snow-covered hills are magnificent, great mountains pure and untouched, summer scars buried under the white blanket.

The woods are often silent with no bird song or sign of life until a flock of tits or finches is encountered, chattering away as they search for seeds. The deer are low down now, seeking forage below the snow line. In hard winters when deep snow covers the glen floors,

many die from starvation. There is little life on the high tops. Just the white ptarmigan flying low across the snowfields and on summits pretty little snow buntings perching hopefully, waiting for the cast-off crumbs from a walker's lunch.

Hard frosts over many days can cause even lowland lochs to freeze, though most are ice-free much of the winter. The high lochans in their cold corries can be frozen for months on end; some, snow-covered, become invisible.

How the snow lies depends on the wind. On rare windless days, snow forms a smooth covering, evening out bumps and hollows. More usually the snow arrives on fierce winds which blow it over the edges of the corries to form huge cornices, great curls of snow hanging over the rocks. The same wind packs the snow into gullies and plasters it over the cliffs.

Streams in the gullies freeze and ice forms on the rocks, attracting ice climbers with their ice axes and crampons. The blown snow ripples across the hills, forming beautiful patterns as it is shaped and sculpted by the wind. This is an entirely different world to that of summer. Harsh, cold and northern; icily beautiful. The cold bites and chills. But soon it will be spring. The cycle never ceases.

Tendrils of cloud creep down the flanks of Braeriach on a freezing winter day.

The long ridge of Sgor Gaoith and Sgoran Dubh Mor viewed from the Fiacaill a' Choire Chais.

A sea of mist fills the glens south of Ben Macdui, with Carn a'Mhaim rising in the foreground.

Mist laps at Ben Macdui and the buttresses of the Devil's Point and Beinn Bhrotain. Beinn a'Ghlo rises in the distance

overleaf The great east face of Cairn Toul,
streaked with snow, seen from Ben Macdui.

The weather station on Cairn Gorm,
encrusted with snow and frost.

Dusk comes early on the mountains in December.
It is 3.30pm on the Cairngorm Plateau looking
towards Beinn Mheadhoin.

Snow-covered hills stretch out to the west from the frozen Cairngorm Plateau.

The icy Fiacaill a' Coire an t-Sneachda etched
against an orange sunset late on a December
afternoon.

After a December sunset, the sky turns pink over
Cairn Gorm.

Cloud rolling in over Braeriach towards Cairn Lochan and Stob Coire an t-Sneachda.

99

Few birds live on the high ground of the Cairngorms due to the harsh conditions. One that does is the snow bunting, a hardy little sparrow-sized bird. Snow buntings can often be seen hopping around popular summits such as Cairn Gorm in search of crumbs from visitors sandwiches, especially in winter when large flocks migrate to the Cairngorms from the arctic. Most return north in spring but some remain to breed on the high tops.

Ptarmigan are small grouse that live on the high plateaux. In summer they have mottled plumage that blends in with the stony terrain, making them hard to see. In winter they turn a brilliant white that makes them stand out when there is no snow.

Winter climbers on the summit of Sgor Gaoith.

The summit of Cairn Lochan at dusk in late December.

The setting sun lights the clouds above the frozen rime and snow encrusted crags of Cairn Lochan.

Late December in Strathspey. Frost coats the meadows and rocks but the patchy snow on the hills shows there has been a mid-winter thaw.

A lone cross-country skier breaks trail through deep snow in the forests of Strathspey.

A waterfall on the Allt Garbhlach crashes down icy slopes in Coire Garbhlach above Glen Feshie.

Sunset over the northern Cairngorms and half-frozen Loch Morlich in January.

The low sun lights up cloud drifting over Braeriach late on a January day.

A January sunset over the cold wind-
rippled waters of Loch Garten.

Christmas Eve: a crescent moon hangs over the last of the sunset above the silhouette of the northern Cairngorms, with the pale line of the River Spey below the hills.

The River Nethy runs out of Strath Nethy between the lower slopes of Bynack More and Cairn Gorm.

A tiny figure stands atop the snowy cliffs of Stob Coire an t-Sneachda.

The hills of the Capel Mounth rise above frozen Loch Muick in the southern Cairngorms.

Loch Einich lies dark and cold below the snow-covered slopes of Braeriach.

FURTHER READING

Highways and Byways in the Central Highlands by Seton Gordon (Macmillian, 1949)

Scotland's Mountains before the Mountaineers by Ian R. Mitchell (Luath Press, 1988)

Legends of the Cairngorms by Affleck Gray (Mainstream, 1988)

The Cairngorms by Adam Watson (SMC, 6th edition 1992)

The Heart of the Cairngorms by Jim Crumley (Colin Baxter, 1997)

On the Trail of Queen Victoria in the Highlands by Ian R. Mitchell (Luath Press, 2000)

The Cairngorm Gateway by Ann Glen (Scottish Cultural Press, 2000).

A High and Lonely Place: The Sanctuary and Plight of the Cairngorms by Jim Crumley (Whittles, 2001)

The Cairngorms by Ronald Turnbull (David & Charles Pevensey Guide, 2002)

Walking in the Cairngorms by Ronald Turnbull (Cicerone, 2005).

Landscape Fashioned By Geology – Cairngorms by John Gordon, Rachel Wignall, Ness Brazier and Patricia Bruneau (Scottish Natural Heritage, 2006)

A Cairngorm Chronicle by A.F. Whyte (Millrace, 2007)

The Life and Times of the Black Pig: A Biography of Ben Macdui by Ronald Turnbull (Millrace, 2007)

The Living Mountain: A Celebration of the Cairngorm Mountains of Scotland by Nan Shepherd (Canongate, 2008)

The Cairngorms Classic Munros by Chris Townsend (Colin Baxter, 2008)

Seton Gordon's Cairngorms edited by Hamish Brown (Whittles, 2009)

A pair of red deer stags in late winter, with their thick cold weather coats just beginning to moult. The knobs that will grow into new antlers can be seen on the stag on the right.

INDEX